A Kid's Guide to the

2018

Winter Games

The World's Greatest Sports Contest

Curious Kids Press • Palm Springs, CA
www.curiouskidspress.com

NOTE: This book was published in August 2017, prior to when most of the USA 2018 Winter Olympic athletes were chosen. For an update on the status of the Team USA athletes competing in the 2018 Winter Games as well as for other 2018 Winter Olympic highlights, be sure to check back regularly at:

www.curiouskidspress.com/Olympics.

Publisher: Curious Kids Press, Palm Springs, CA 92264.
Designed by: Michael Owens
Editor: Sterling Moss
Copy Editor: Janice Ross

Table of Contents

OLYMPIC OATH

AT THE BEGINNING of every Olympic Games, one athlete from the host nation is chosen to take the Olympic Oath on behalf of all athletes at the Games. The oath taker holds a corner of the Olympic flag while taking the oath below.

"In the name of all competitors, I promise that we shall take part in these Olympic Games, respecting and abiding by the rules that govern them, committing ourselves to a sport without doping and without drugs, in the true spirit of sportsmanship, for the glory of sport and the honor of our teams."

Welcome to the 2018 Winter Games

ON FEBRUARY 9, 2018, more than 2,500 athletes from at least 79 countries around the world will gather in PyeongChang, South Korea, for the XXIII Olympic Winter Games.

More than a billion people from around the world will be watching the 16-day event. Who will take home an Olympic medal? It's anyone's guess. But to help you get ready for this exciting event, this book includes a lot of fun facts and trivia about the history of the Winter Games, as well as information about each of the three Winter Olympic sports and 15 disciplines.

In addition, the book also includes a special Who to Watch section for each discipline, spotlighting a Team USA athlete who we think has a good chance of taking home a medal.

So, get ready for all the exciting action and events at the world's greatest winter sports contest -- the 2018 Winter Olympics. Enjoy.

The Olympic Rings

The five Olympic rings represent the five major regions of the world -- the Americas, Europe, Africa, Asia, and Oceania -- and every national flag in the world includes one of the five colors (blue, yellow, black, green, and red).

2018 Winter Olympics Medal Tracker
To help you keep track of Team USA's medals in each event, turn to page 54 for the 2018 Winter Olympics Medal Tracker.

Where in the World Is PyeongChang

PYEONGCHANG (SAY: PIE-AWN-CHANG) IS A CITY in the Republic of Korea (aka South Korea). It is in the northern part of the country about 110 miles (180 km) east of Seoul, the capital of South Korea.

The country is in East Asia. It borders North Korea and is surrounded by water on three sides.

The population of PyeongChang is about 43,000. Its area is 562 sq. mi (1,463 sq. km) or about as big as Phoenix, Arizona.

PyeongChang's slogan is "Happy 700 PyeongChang." That's because the city's average elevation (or height above sea level) is about 700m (2,296 feet). Some people say that a high elevation is the best environment for human life, which makes PyeongChang one of the healthiest places in the world to live.

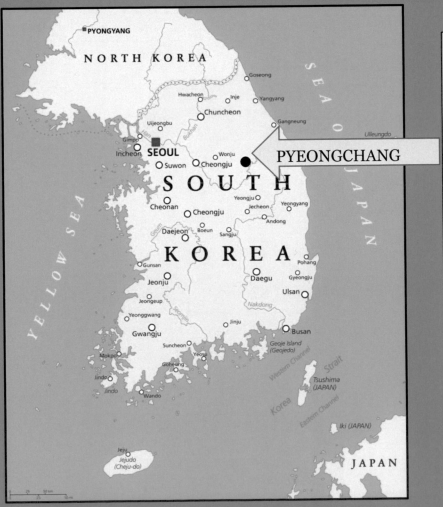

What Time Is It in PyeongChang?

Would you like to know what time it is in PyeongChang? It's easy. Follow these two steps:

1. Check the Coordinated Universal Time.* (Visit: https://time.is/UTC)

2. Add 9 hours to that time.

That's the time in South Korea.

* Coordinated Universal Time is the standard time by which the world regulates (or sets) its clocks and time.

Winter Games
Where They've Been Held

QUICK QUIZ: How many times do you think the Winter Games have been held in the United States since 1924? 7? 5? 4? Take a guess. Then, look at the list below to find the answer.

1924: Chamonix, FRANCE

1928: St. Moritz, SWITZERLAND

1932: Lake Placid, NY, UNITED STATES

1936: Garmisch-Partenkirchen, GERMANY

1940: Canceled

1944: Canceled

1948: St. Moritz, SWITZERLAND

1952: Oslo, NORWAY

1956: Cortina d'Ampezzo, ITALY

1960: Squaw Valley, CA, UNITED STATES

1964: Innsbruck, AUSTRIA

1968: Grenoble, FRANCE

1972: Sapporo, JAPAN

1976: Innsbruck, AUSTRIA

1980: Lake Placid, NY, UNITED STATES

1984: Sarajevo, YUGOSLOVIA

1988: Calgary, Alberta, CANADA

1992: Albertville, FRANCE

1994: Lillehammer, NORWAY

1998: Nagano, JAPAN

2002: Salt Lake City, UT, UNITED STATES

2006: Torino (Turin), ITALY

2010: Vancouver, BC, CANADA

2014: Sochi, RUSSIA

2018: PyeongChang, SOUTH KOREA

Winter Games: Then and Now

	1924 Chamonix, France	2018 PyeongChang
No. of Nations	16	At least 79
No. of Participants	258	About 3,000
No. of Sports/Events	6 sports	102 events

A Brief History of the Winter Olympics

THE YEAR WAS 1924. A total of 258 athletes (247 men and 11 women) from 16 countries gathered in Chamonix, France, to compete in 16 winter sports events. It marked the official beginning of the Winter Olympics.

Twenty-eight years earlier in 1896 the first modern Olympic games were held in Athens, Greece. The events were all summer sports.

In 1908, a figure skating event was added to the summer games, and in 1920 ice hockey joined figure skating as an official Olympic event.

At the 1924 Winter Olympics, Norway won the most medals. At the end of the 2014 Winter Olympics, Norway was still the country with the most Winter Olympic medals. The country's athletes had collected 329 medals, 47 more than the U.S.

Charles Jewtraw

On January 26, 1924, Charles Jewtraw from New York became the first person to win a gold medal in a Winter Olympics event. He won the gold medal in the 500-meter speed skating event. It was the only gold medal that Americans won that year.

1904

For the first time, gold, silver, and bronze medals are awarded at the Olympic Games.

1924

The first official Winter Games are held in St. Moritz, France. (Before 1924, ice skating and ice hockey were part of the Summer Olympics.)

1932

Eddie Eagan becomes the first American to win a gold medal in both the summer and winter Olympic games. He won a gold medal in boxing at the summer Olympics in 1920. Then, this year (1932), he won a gold medal for bobsleigh. Today, he is still the only American athlete who has won a gold medal in both summer and winter Olympics.

1936

Canadian athlete Diana Gordon Lennox competes in the slalom and downhill alpine skiing event – with one arm in a plaster cast!

1940 - 1944

The 1940 Winter Olympic Games were scheduled to take place in Sapporo, Japan. They were canceled, however, due to the onset (or beginning) of World War II. Four years later, the Winter Games were also canceled due to the war.

1948

Dick Button becomes the first American figure skater to win gold at the Winter Oympics. He was also the first to land a double axel in Olympic competition.

1956

Tenley Albright becomes the first American woman to win a gold medal in figure skating at the Winter Olympics. As a child, Tenley had polio, a disease that can cause people to lose the use of their arms or legs.

1960

For the first time since 1924, the bobsleigh event is not included in the Winter Olympics. The organizing committee in Squaw Valley, where the Games were held, wanted to reduce expenses by not building a bobsleigh track.

1968

For the first time in Olympic history, athletes are tested for drugs. No one failed.

1972

Sapporo, Japan, becomes the first Asian city to host the Winter Olympic Games.

1976

Winter Games are supposed to be held in Denver, CO. But Denver voters vote against the use of public funds for the Games. So the Games are moved to Innsbruck, Austria.

1980

The American hockey team wins the gold medal in a stunning upset over the Soviet Union. It's called the Miracle on Ice. The Soviet Union had won the gold medal in six of the seven previous Winter Olympic games and were the favorites to win once more.

1984

Phil Mahre and twin brother Steve (younger by 4 minutes) win gold and silver medals in slalom.

1992

This was the last time the Winter Olympics and Summer Olympics were held in the same year. The next Winter Games were held in 1994 and then every four years after that. The next Summer Games were held in 1996 and every four years after that.

1988

A bobsleigh team from the Caribbean island of Jamaica makes their nation's Winter Olympic debut. Originally, the team practiced in a pushcart on a flat surface on a military base in Jamaica. In the two-man event, they finished 30th overall.

1998

American figure skater Tara Lipinski becomes the youngest Olympic Gold Medalist in an *individual* event in the Winter Olympics. She was 15 years, 255 days old.

2002

American bobsledder Vonetta Flowers becomes the first African-American athlete to win a gold medal at the Winter Games. She won the gold medal with her teammate Jill Bakken.

2014

Twelve new events make their debut at the 2014 Winter Olympics, including women's ski jumping

2018

Three countries – Eritrea, Kosovo, and Malaysia -- compete in the Winter Olympics for the first time.

The Olympic Torch Relay: An Olympic Tradition

THE TORCH RELAY has been an important part of every Olympic games since the Summer Olympics in 1936 in Berlin, Germany.

The relay begins several months before the start of the Olympics in Olympia, Greece, where the torch is lit.

It then goes to the host nation where it travels to cities or provinces throughout the country, carried by thousands of torchbearers. At each stop along the way, there are fun events and activities scheduled.

The torch finally arrives at the Olympic stadium in the host city.

The final torchbearer (or possibly torchbearers) race into the stadium to light the Olympic cauldron with the flame. The cauldron remains lit during the games and is extinguished (or put out) at the Closing Ceremony of the Games.

Olympic Cauldron:

A specially designed pot that sits on a pedestal, which is also specially designed, and holds the Olympic flame during the Olympic Games.

Many famous athletes have had the honor of being the last runner in the Olympic Torch Relay and the honor of lighting the Olympic cauldron at the opening ceremony, including former heavyweight boxing champion Muhammad Ali in 1996.

Who will be the final torchbearer in 2018? It's a well-guarded secret. But our money is on figure skater Yuna Kim from South Korea. She was a gold medal winner at the 2010 Winter Olympics and won silver in 2014.

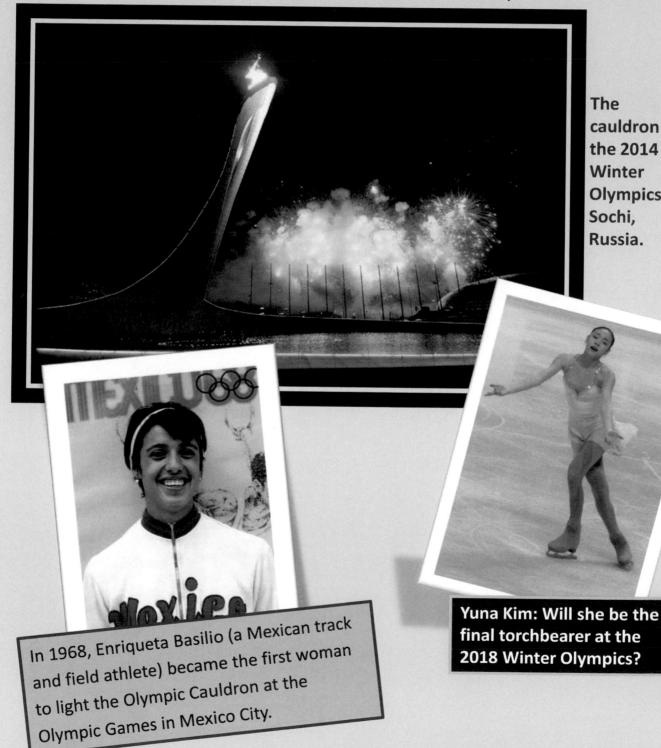

The cauldron at the 2014 Winter Olympics in Sochi, Russia.

In 1968, Enriqueta Basilio (a Mexican track and field athlete) became the first woman to light the Olympic Cauldron at the Olympic Games in Mexico City.

Yuna Kim: Will she be the final torchbearer at the 2018 Winter Olympics?

Winter Events

THE WINTER GAMES consist of three Olympic sports: **snow sports**, **ice sports**, and **sliding sports**. Within the three Olympic sports, there are fifteen different sport "disciplines." And within those disciplines, there are 102 different events and 102 gold medals.

The sport with the largest number of Olympic disciplines is snow sports. There are seven disciplines. Look at the chart below. How many sports disciplines are in Ice Sports? Sliding Sports?

	Snow Sports	Ice Sports	Sliding Sports
No. of Disciplines	7	5	3
No. of Gold Medals	61	32	9
Olympic Disciplines	Alpine Skiing	Curling	Bobsleigh
	Biathlon	Figure Skating	Luge
	Cross-country Skiing	Ice Hockey	Skeleton
	Freestyle Skiing	Short Track	
	Nordic Combined	Speed Skating	
	Ski Jumping		
	Snowboard		

Olympic Fact File

American speed skater Apolo Anton Ohno has won more medals in the Winter Olympic events than any other athlete. He has a total of 8 medals in short track speed skating -- two gold, two silver, and four bronze.

SNOW Sports

SNOW SPORTS AT THE 2018 WINTER OLYMPICS consist of seven disciplines. (See the list in the chart below.)

At the 2014 Winter Olympics, U.S. athletes took home 17 medals in snow sports – 8 Gold, 3 Silver, and 6 Bronze.. Will they beat that record at the 2018 Olympics. Use the chart to keep track.

DISCIPLINE	GOLD		SILVER		BRONZE		TOTAL	
	2014	2018	2014	2018	2014	2018	2014	2018
Alpine Skiing	2		1		2		5	
Biathlon	0		0		0		0	
Cross-country Skiing	0		0		0		0	
Freestyle Skiing	3		2		2		7	
Nordic Combined	0		0		0		0	
Ski Jumping	0		0		0		0	
Snowboard	3		0		2		5	
TOTAL	8		3		6		17	

ALPINE SKIING

IMAGINE SKIING DOWNHILL at a speed of up to 87 mph (140 km/hr) in a long, steep slope downward.

Or making sharp turns through "gates," in a shorter, but still challenging course.

Those are just two of the thrilling events in the Alpine Skiing discipline.

Alpine Skiing At-a-Glance

Year It Became Olympic Event: 1936
Number of Events in 2018: 11
U.S. Medals Won in 2014: 5
Country with Most Medals: Austria (114)

11 Alpine Skiing Events

Alpine Combined (Men and Women)
Downhill (Men and Women)
Giant Slalom (Men and Women)
Slalom (Men and Women)
Super-G (Men and Women)
Alpine Team Mixed: NEW 2018

Did You Know?

Alpine Skiing events are basically divided into two categories: speed events, including downhill and super giant slalom (or super-G) and technical events, including slalom and giant slalom.

The Alpine Team Mixed is the newest Alpine Skiing event. It consists of two men and two women.

In the 2014 Winter Games, Mikaela took home gold in the slalom event. Can she do it again?

WHO TO WATCH!

Mikaela Shiffrin

Born: March 13, 1995
Birthplace: Vail, CO
Hobbies: Playing tennis and soccer

WHEN MIKAELA WAS 18 YEARS, 345 days old, she made Olympic history. She became the youngest athlete (male or female) to win an Olympic slalom gold medal. Maybe that shouldn't be too surprising. After all, Mikaela has been skiing almost since the time she could walk. Keep your eye on Mikaela in the slalom and giant slalom events. Odds are high she'll be on the podium.

"Being a great skier was always my DREAM."

WHAT DO YOU GET when you combine cross-country skiing with rifle shooting? The answer is a rather insane Olympic event called *biathlon* (bi-ath-lon). The word biathlon is Greek meaning two tests. And there are definitely two tests in the Winter Olympics biathlon event.

Biathlon At-a-Glance

Year It Became Olympic Event: 1960 (men's); 1992 (women's)

Number of Events in 2018: 11

U.S. Medals Won in 2014: 0

Country with the Most Medals: Germany (45)

11 Biathlon Events
Sprint (Men and Women)
Pursuit (Men and Women)
Individual (Men and Women)
Mass Start (Men and Women)
Relay (Men and Women)
Mixed Relay

During a biathlon race, athletes ski across more than 12 miles of snow-covered ground until they reach a shooting range. They then stop, and shoot at metal targets. Sometimes the athletes are standing; sometime they are lying down. The goal? To complete the course in the least amount of time, while hitting as many targets as possible.

Olympic Fact File
Biathlon is the only Winter Sports discipline in which the U.S. has never won a medal. Will that change in 2018?

Susan Dunklee

WHO TO WATCH!

Born: February 13, 1986
Birthplace: Barton, VT
Hobbies: Hiking, Jigsaw puzzles, gardening, reading

WHEN SUSAN WAS TWO YEARS OLD, she learned to ski. When she was 22 years old, she learned to shoot. So is there any wonder why she is a top athlete in biathlon? In February 2017, she finished 2nd in the Mass Start in the 2017 Biathlon World Championships, making her the first American woman to win an individual medal at World Championships in biathlon. Can she do it again at the Winter Olympics. We're betting the answer is yes.

UPDATE: In 2017, Susan became the first U.S. woman (and second U.S. athlete) to qualify for the 2018 Winter Olympic Games.

"The most important thing is to keep my *focus* on performing well and controlling what is within my power. The results will take care of themselves."

Cross-Country Skiing

CROSS-COUNTRY SKIING offers a lot of health benefits. But does it make walking on the moon easier? Harrison Schmitt, a crewmember of the space shuttle Apollo 17, thought so. In fact, he thought that astronauts heading to the moon should learn the art of cross-country skiing before they blast-off for the moon. He believed that the techniques in skiing would be helpful in walking on the moon. Anybody ready for a lunar skiing holiday?

Cross-country Skiing At-a-Glance

Year It Became Olympic Event: 1924 (men's); 1952 (women's)

Number of Events in 2018: 12

U.S. Medals Won in 2014: 0

Country with the Most Medals: Norway (107)

12 Cross-country Events
Individual (Men and Women)
Skiathlon (Men and Women)
Sprint (Men and Women)
Team Sprint (Men and Women)
Mass Start (Men and Women)
Relay (Men and Women)

Did You Know?
The word "ski" is a Norwegian word meaning "a long length of wood."

WHO TO WATCH!

Jessie Diggins

Born: August 26, 1991
Birthplace: Afton, MN
Hobbies: Reading, camping, canoeing, playing violin

JESSIE KNOWS what it's like to be first. She was part of the first-ever U.S. team to win a World Cup team sprint event (with Kikkan Randall). She was also the first U.S. cross-country skier to win a world championship gold medal (with Randall in team sprint). Can she add to those "firsts" at the 2018 Olympics? We think so.

"It doesn't take a hero to be happy when you're on the podium. But it does take a hero...to handle a disappointing race or unexpected crash with **sportsmanship**."

Freestyle Skiing

BACK FLIPS, TWISTS, BREATHTAKING JUMPS 20 ft. (6 m) into the air: It might make you think you're at a gymnastics event. But it's all part of the artistry of freestyle skiing — sometimes called a circus on the snow.

Skier performing an aerial.

Freestyle Skiing At-a-Glance

Year It Became Olympic Event: 1992
Number of Events in 2018: 10
U.S. Medals Won in 2014: 7
Country with Most Medals: United States (21)

Olympic Fact File
As of the 2014 Olympics, the United States has won more medals in FREESTYLE SKIING than any other country.

WHO **TO WATCH!**

Gus Kenworthy

Born: October 1, 1991
Birthplace: London, England
Hobbies: Skateboarding, jumping on the trampoline, and "chasing snow throughout the year."

GUS IS ALMOST AS FAMOUS AS a dog-lover as he is for his extraordinary freestyle skiing talent. At the 2014 Winter Olympics in SochiRussia – where he won a silver medal -- he stayed behind after the Games. He was determined to save a family of stray dogs – four puppies and their mother -- and to bring attention to the stray dog problem in Sochi. Can he turn Sochi silver into PyeongChang gold. With determination like this, we have no doubt.

"When it snows, you have two choices: shovel or ski."

Nordic Combined

EVERYONE AGREES that it's one of the hardest ski events at the Winter Olympics. It's an event that combines cross-country skiing with ski jumping. How hard is that? In a way, it's like a swimmer competing in a high dive, and then immediately follow that with a 5000-meter race. Whoa! There is no women's event in Nordic Combined. It's the only Olympic discipline to remain "men-only." Will that change in the future? We think so.

Nordic Combined At-a-Glance
Year It Became Olympic Event: 1994
Number of Events in 2018: 3
U.S. Medals Won, 2014: 0
Country with the Most Medals: Norway (30)

3 Nordic Combined Events

Individual (ski jumping normal hill + 10km cross-country skiing)

Individual (ski jumping large hill + 10km cross-country skiing)

Team Competition

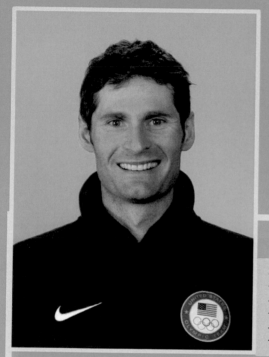

WHO TO WATCH!
Bryan Fletcher

Born: June 27, 1986
Birthplace: Steamboat Springs, CO
Hobbies: Camping, kayaking, cooking

IT'S NOT SURPRISING that Bryan is a skier. After all, he was born in Steamboat Springs, or, as he puts it, "a ski town through and through." What may come as a surprise is that Bryan is a cancer survivor. When he was almost three years old, he was diagnosed with a form of cancer called Leukemia. Then, while being treated for cancer, he started ski jumping and Nordic Combined. "I was hooked from day one," he says. "It's what kept my spirits alive." And over the years, he worked hard to develop his skill. Can he bring home gold from PyeongChang? He's one of the best Nordic Combined skiers in the world. So there's no reason why not.

"As long as I have **balance** between training and family life, I am happy and the results will come."

SKi JUMPiNG

Ski Jumping At-a-Glance
Year It Became Olympic Event: 1924 (men); 2014 (women)
Number of Events in 2018: 4
U.S. Medals Won, 2014: 0
Country with the Most Medals: Norway (30)

WOMEN HAVE BEEN SKI JUMPING for as long anyone can remember -- just not at the Olympics. Ever since the first Winter Olympics, ski jumping was limited just to men. Officials felt that women's bodies were too, well, "fragile."

That finally changed in 2011 when the International Olympic Committee (IOC) announced that a women's ski jumping event would be added to the 2014 Winter Games. But there is still only one ski jumping event for women; there are three ski jumping events for men.

What's it like to ski jump? American ski jumper Lindsey Van once said, "It's as if you can fly. It's a feeling like nothing else."

4 Ski Jumping Events

Men's Normal Hill Individual
Ladies' Normal Hill Individual
Men's Large Hill Individual
Men's Team

Did You Know?

As of 2017, the official record for the longest ski jump was 831 ft. (253.5 m). That's like flying the length of nearly two and a half American football fields. Austrian ski jumper Stefan Kraft set the record in March 2017.

WHO TO WATCH!

Born: August 1, 1994
Birthplace: Salt Lake City, UT
Hobbies: Biking, reading, soccer

Sarah Hendrickson

SKI JUMPING IS A FAMILY TRADITION in Sarah's family. Both her father and brother are ski jumpers. Sarah herself has won more medals than almost any other female ski jumper in history. In 2014, she became the first woman ever to jump in a ski jumping event at the Winter Olympics. But, then, after a serious knee injury, she had to take 18 months off. She's back now, ready to fly again. But can she make history at the 2018 Olympic Winter Games? We bet she can.

"It's easy to get **overwhelmed** by the future, but if you stop, breathe, and do what you can in the moment, that is all you can control."

Snowboard

Snowboard At-a-Glance

Year It Became Olympic Event: 1998
Number of Events in 2018: 10
U.S. Medals Won, 2014: 5
Country with
the Most Medals:
United States (24)

YOU NEVER KNOW what might happen at the Winter Games. Take, for example, the 2014 Winter Games in Sochi, Russia. Jamie Anderson was in fifth place heading into her final run. But guess what happened? She made a flawless run and soared to victory. She became the first-ever women's Olympic Slopestyle gold medalist. Who will make Olympic history in PyeongChang?

10 Snowboard Events
Parallel Giant Slalom (Men and Women)
Halfpipe (Men and Women)
Snowboard Cross (Men and Women)
Big Air (Men and Women) NEW in 2018
Slopestyle (Men and Women)

WHO TO WATCH!

Jamie Anderson

Born: September 13, 1990
Birthplace: South Lake Tahoe, CA
Hobbies: Biking, hiking, yoga, dancing

JAMIE HAS BEEN RIDING since she was nine years old. In 2006, when Jamie was only 15 years old, she made history when she became the youngest-ever Winter X-Games medalist in history. She won bronze. Since then, she has added nine more Winter X-Games to her total, including another bronze, four silver, and four gold. In 2014 at the Winter Games in Sochi, Russia, Jamie made history again by becoming the first ever women's Olympic slopestyle gold medalist. Can she add to her medals in 2018 Winter Olympics? What do you think?

"I think with anything in life, we all have the **power**. It's a matter of tapping into it and really believing in yourself."

Olympic Fact File
As of the 2014 Olympics, the United States has won more medals in SNOWBOARD than any other country.

(NOTE: The Winter X- Games is a major winter sports competition organized by ESPN every year.)

WHO TO WATCH!

Alex Deibold

Born: May 8, 1986
Birthplace: New Haven, CT.
Current Home: Boulder, CO
Hobbies: Biking, surfing, backpacking, golf.

ALEX'S FIRST WINTER OLYMPICS GAMES was in 2010 in Vancouver, BC, Canada. But he wasn't there as an athlete. He was a wax tech (waxing boards for the riders). "It was hard work," he says, "but I learned a lot."

Four years later at the 2014 Olympic Winter Games, Alex took home a bronze medal in men's snowboard cross. More recently, at the 2016-2017 FIS Snowboard World Cup, he finished second in the men's snowboard cross. Not bad for a wax tech.

FIS = International Ski Federation

"It's great to support your teammates," Alex says about his time as a wax tech. "But I was jealous that they got to participate in this **awesome spectacle** that is the Olympics."

Ice Sports

ICE SPORTS AT THE 2018 WINTER OLYMPICS consist of five disciplines. At the 2014 Winter Olympics, U.S. athletes took home four medals in ice sports – 1 gold, 2 silver, and 1 bronze. Will they beat that record at the 2018 Olympics? Use the chart to keep track.

DISCIPLINE	GOLD 2014	GOLD 2018	SILVER 2014	SILVER 2018	BRONZE 2014	BRONZE 2018	TOTAL 2014	TOTAL 2018
Curling	0		0		0		0	
Figure Skating	1		0		1		2	
Hockey	0		1		0		1	
Speedskating	0		0		0		0	
Short Track	0		1		0		1	
TOTAL	1		2		1		4	

Ice Sports
Curling

Curling At-a-Glance
Year It Became Olympic Event: 1998
Number of Events in 2018: 3
U.S. Medals Won, 2014: 0
Country with the Most Medals: Canada (10)

SOME PEOPLE THINK that curling is the silliest sport ever invented. Imagine: You slide "stones," called rocks, on a sheet of ice towards a circular target area, called a house. At the same time, two teammates use curling brooms to sweep the ice surface in the path of the stone. Sounds silly, right? But the truth is curling is a game that requires a lot of strategy and teamwork. That's why curling is sometimes called "chess on ice." Are you ready to give it a try?

Did You Know?
Curling is Scotland's national winter sport.

3 Curling Events
Men's Curling
Women's Curling
Mixed Doubles Curling NEW 2018

Talk about Good Sportsmanship!

In curling, if a player accidentally touches a stone with his or her broom or body part (called *burning* a stone), that player is expected to call his/her own infraction (or breaking of a rule). It's just good sportsmanship.

"My motivation really comes from trying to be the best and having teammates that do the same."

WHO TO WATCH!

John Shuster

Nickname: Shoostie
Born: November 3, 1982
Hometown: Chisholm, MN
Resides: Superior, WI
Position: Skip (or captain)

JOHN STARTED CURLING in 1997. Since then, he has competed in three Olympic Winter Games – 2006 in Torino, Italy (bronze), 2010 in Vancouver, BC, Canada, (10th), and 2014 in Sochi, Russia (9th). While American curlers in general haven't done too well in the last two Winter Olympics, Shuster and his teammates won the 2017 U.S. National Championships, and came in 4th in the 2017 World Championships. They're set to take the podium in PyeongChang.

Short Track

Short Track At-a-Glance
Year It Became Olympic Event: 1988
Number of Events in 2018: 8
U.S. Medals Won, 2014: 1
Country with the Most Medals: South Korea (42)

IT'S OFTEN CALLED NASCAR ON ICE. And for good reason. Short Track requires strategy, bravery, and skill, all rolled into one of the most thrilling of all Olympic winter sports.

So what's the difference between short track and speed skating? Lots. For one thing, in speed skating, athletes are racing against the clock. In Short Track, athletes are racing against each other around a shorter track. Crashes happen a lot.

8 Short Track Events

Men Individual: 500m, 1000m, 1500m

Men's Team Relay: 5000m

Ladies Individual: 500m, 1000m, 1500m

Ladies Team Relay: 3000m

Olympic Snapshot

J.R. didn't get to compete in the 2006 Winter Olympics. Do you know why? He missed the minimum age requirement by 17 days.

Born: July 17, 1990
Hometown: Federal Way, WA
Hobbies: Golfing, cycling, traveling

WHO TO WATCH!

J. R. Celski

J.R. started out as an in-line skater. And he was a national champion in that. But then he saw the 2002 Winter Olympics and decided that's really what he wanted to do. And he's been doing it in a big way ever since. He already has a couple of Olympic bronze medals and a silver medal – bronze from the 2010 Olympic Winter Games (1500 m and 5000m relay) and silver from the 2014 Olympic Winter Games (5000m relay). Can he add gold to his collection? We're bettin' on him.

"I thank God for BLESSING me with the opportunity to pursue what I love."

Speed Skating

Speed Skating At-a-Glance

Year It Became Olympic Event: 1924
 (men); 1960 (women)

Number of Events in 2018: 14

U.S. Medals Won: 2014: 0

Country with the Most Medals: Netherlands (105)

IN WHAT OLYMPIC WINTER SPORT have U.S. athletes won more medals than any other? If you said "Speed Skating," you're right. By the end of the Sochi 2014 Games, U.S. speed skaters at all Winter Olympics had won 67 medals. How many will they add to that number in PyeongChang in 2018?

14 Speed Skating Events

Men's	Women's
500 m	500 m
1000 m	1000 m
1500 m	1500 m
5000 m	3000 m
10,000 m	5000 m
Mass Start NEW 2018	Mass Start NEW 2018
Team Pursuit	Team Pursuit

"I'm much more CONFIDENT [now], but you never know what's going to happen in the next race, so I have to keep working hard towards what I want."

Born: March 20, 1989

Birthplace/Hometown: High Point, NC

Hobbies: Volleyball and softball

Fun Fact: Wants to go to dental school after speedskating.

WHO TO WATCH!

Heather Bergsma

Heather has won a bunch of medals recently. At the 2017 World Single Distance Championships, she won gold in 1000 metre , gold in 1500 metre gold, and bronze in Mass Start. She was also the overall silver medalist in the 2017 World Sprint Championships. Can she win gold in PyeongChang? Some say she actually has a chance to win more medals than any other athlete at the 2018 games. "She makes it look easy," says her coach. But, he adds, that's because of the training and preparation and dedication she has for the sport. Keep your eye on Heather, for sure.

Ice Hockey

Ice Hockey At-a-Glance

Year It Became Olympic Event: 1920 (men); 1998 (women)

U.S. Medals Won, 2014: 1

Country with the Most Medals: Canada (20)

HOCKEY GREAT PHIL KESSEL made big news at the 2014 Winter Olympics for doing something no American had done in a Winter Olympics ice hockey tournament since 2002. Can you guess what that was? He scored a hard-to-get hat trick for the U.S. Will the U.S. team do it again this year? It's anybody's guess.

Did You Know
The word hockey comes from a French word (hocquet), meaning stick.

WHO TO WATCH!

Jocelyne Lamoureux-Davidson

Born: July 3, 1989
Birthplace/Hometown: Grand Forks, ND
Position: Forward

Monique Lamoureux-Morando

Born: July 3, 1989
Birthplace/Hometown: Grand Forks, ND
Position: Defender

(c)2014 USOC

AS TEENAGERS, Jocelyne and Monique were both all-state in ice hockey. They were also both named to the United States women's national ice hockey team for the 2010 and 2014 winter Olympics – and ended up walking away both times with a silver medal. Can they make it gold at the 2018 Games? We hope so.

(c)2014 USOC

Olympics Fact Box
Jocelyne and Monique are the first set of twins ever to play hockey at the Olympics.

"If [Jocelyne] is maybe not feeling it one day, or I'm not feeling it another day, we'll both get on each other and say, 'We have to get going.' It's basically like having a **TRAINING** partner 24/7."-- **Monique**

Figure Skating

FIGURE SKATING is the oldest sport on the Winter Games program. It was first contested in 1908 at the London Summer games. (Winter Games as a separate event didn't officially begin until 1924.)

Today, figure skating is one of the most popular sports to watch on TV. It's artistic, graceful, and quite thrilling. It also requires a great deal of skill.

Figure Skating At-a-Glance

Year It Became Olympic Event: 1908

No. of Events in 2018: 5

U.S Medals Won, 2014: 2

Country with the Most Medals: United States (49)

5 Figure Skating Events

Men's singles
Ladies' singles
Pair skating
Ice dancing
Team

WHO TO WATCH!

Nathan
Chen

Born: May 5, 1999

Birthplace: Salt Lake City, UT

Hometown: Irvine, CA

Hobbies: Playing guitar, biking

HE'S BEEN CALLED the new king of American Figure Skating. And no wonder. Nathan has done things on the ice that nobody ever thought was possible. Like landing a not-to-be-believed five clean quads in competition in 2017. Nathan began skating at the age of 3, and by 17 became the youngest U.S. man to medal at the Figure Skating Grand Prix.

"There are a lot of **cultural** differences between Americans and Chinese, and I think that having both aspects be part of my life has helped me in a lot of ways, from an academic standpoint to an athletics standpoint."

WHO TO WATCH!

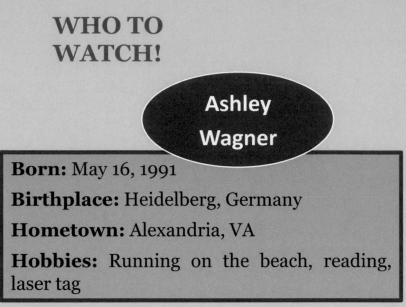

Ashley Wagner

Born: May 16, 1991

Birthplace: Heidelberg, Germany

Hometown: Alexandria, VA

Hobbies: Running on the beach, reading, laser tag

ASHLEY HAS BEEN SKATING since she was five years old. But in 1998, when she was seven years old, she watched American figure skater Tara Lipinski win the gold medal at the 1998 Winter Olympics in Japan. From that moment, she decided that she wanted to complete in the Olympics. And she achieved that goal in 2014 at the Winter Olympics in Sochi, Russia. She won a bronze medal in the team event. In 2018 she will be going for gold.

"My PASSION is what fuels me. I'm here because I've worked hard to be here. That's something I'm proud of."

SLiDiNG SporTS

SLIDING SPORTS AT THE 2018 WINTER OLYMPICS consist of three disciplines: bobsleigh (aka bobsled), luge, and skeleton. At the 2014 Winter Olympics, U.S. athletes took home seven medals in sliding sports —two silver and five bronze. Will they beat that record at the 2018 Olympics? Use the chart to keep track.

DISCIPLINE	GOLD		SILVER		BRONZE		TOTAL	
	2014	2018	2014	2018	2014	2018	2014	2018
Bobsleigh	0		1		3		4	
Luge	0		0		1		1	
Skeleton	0		1		1		2	
TOTAL	0		2		5		7	

BobSleigH

YEARS AGO, athletes on a sled developed the habit of "bobbing" their head back and forth to help make the sled go faster. Truth: It didn't really do much good, but the name stuck, and today we have the thrilling sport of bobsleigh.

Bobsleigh At-a-Glance

Year It Became Olympic Event: 1924 (4-man); 1932 (2-man); 2002 (women's)
Number of Events in 2018: 3
U.S. Medals Won, 2014: 4
Country with the Most Medals: Switzerland (31)

3 Bobsleigh Events
4-man bobsleigh
2-man bobsleigh
Women's bobsleigh

Bobsleigh from about 1910

WHO TO WATCH!

Elana
Meyers
Taylor

Born: October 10, 1984

Birthplace: Oceanside, CA

Future Goal: To become head of the U.S. Olympic Committee

ELANA BEGAN THE SPORT of bobsled in 2007. By 2010, she had won a bronze medal at the Winter Olympics as a brakeman with partner Erin Pac. She moved into the driver's seat after the 2010 Olympics, and in 2014 she claimed the 2014 Olympic silver medal as a driver with Lauryn Williams. Today, she is considered one of the best – if not *the* best – female drivers. Keep your eye on Elana.

"I love trying new things, and I really think that's how you're going to get to where you want to go in life by being open to new things and being open to new **experiences**."

Luge

Luge At-a-Glance
Year It Became Olympic Event: 1964
Number of Events in 2018: 4
U.S. Medals Won, 2014: 1
Country with the Most Medals: Germany (31)

IMAGINE lying flat on your back on a tiny sled. Your feet are stretched out in front of you. And you're zooming down an icy hill with twists and turns at speeds up to 90 miles per hour (140 kph). Oh, yeah, there's one other thing. You don't have any brakes! Yikes!

If that sounds like fun, then you're ready for **luge** – one of the oldest winter sports at the Olympics. Athletes who compete in luge events are known as lugers. They use their legs and shoulders to steer down the 2,018 metre track .

4 Luge Events
Men's Singles
Women's Singles
Doubles (2 men; 2 women; or man and woman)
Team Relay

Chris Mazdzer

Born: June 26, 1988

Birthplace: Saranac Lake, NY

Hobbies: Rock climbing, mountain biking

CHRIS IS A TOTAL outdoorsman. He loves rock climbing, mountain biking, and just simply exploring the world. He's been sliding since he was 8 years old, and was asked to travel with Junior nationals when he was 13. He's alo a two-time Olympian – in 2010 in Vancouver, Canada, and in 2014 in Sochi, Russia. On both occasions he finished 13th. Will he make it to the Olympic medal platform in 2018? We're rootin' for him.

*"I've **failed** a lot of times, but each failure helped me to realize what I wanted to do."*

Olympic Facts File
The last time the U.S. won a gold medal in a luge event was in 2002.

Did You Know? Lugers wear spiked gloves which they use on the surface of the ice to gain extra acceleration (or speed) as they start the race down the hill.

SKeLeToN

Skeleton At-a-Glance

Year It Became Olympic Event: 2002

Number of Events in 2018: 2

U.S. Medals Won, 2014: 2

Country with Most Medals: United States (8)

PICTURE THIS: You get a running start from the opening gate, jump head-first on a tiny sled, and then slide down a track of artificial ice 1,500m long – reaching speeds of 75 mph (120 kph). Whew! Sound like fun? Or simply scary?

Skeleton was first contested at the 2nd Winter Games in St. Moritz, France, in 1928 and then again in 1948. After that, it was excluded from the Olympic program. Why? Officials felt the sport was simply too dangerous. Nevertheless, it was brought back in 2002.

WHO TO WATCH!

Katie Uhlaender

Born: July 17, 1984
Birthplace: Vail, CO
Fun Fact: She owns beef cattle.

Katie has won a slew of medals in her career as an American skeleton racer, including 11 World Cup medals, six silver medals, and a trio of bronze medals. At the 2014 Winter Olympics, she missed the podium by four-hundredths of a second. You can hardly blink in that amount of time. "I'm not going to lie," Katie said at the time. "It's devastating." Can she reach the podium in PyeongChang in 2018? We're pulling for her.

"Being an Olympian is a huge **honor**. But the biggest honor is representing my country. I take a huge amount of pride in that."

Did You Know? The body temperature of an athlete in the skeleton event must be within a certain temperature range before the athlete can compete. Why? Heat makes skeleton sleds go faster. So heating the sled is against the rules – as is a hot body.

Hope you ENJOYED reading about the 2018 Winter Olympics.
Please leave a review of this book at Amazon.com. Thank you!
To help you keep track of the medals Team USA wins during the 2018 Winter Olympics, turn to the Medal Tracker starting on page 54.

Olympic Sports Terms

SNOW SPORTS

Skiing

Aerial Skiing: A type of skiing in which athletes ski off a 2-4 meter jump that propels (or pushes) them up to 20 feet (about 6 meters) in the air where they perform multiple flips and twists.

Alpine Skiing: Downhill skiing.

Cross-country Skiing: Skiing on a flat surface on skis that are thinner than downhill skis.

Freestyle Skiing: A type of skiing that consists of skiers performing a variety of twists and flips, often 40 to 50 feet (12-15 meters) in the air.

Half-Pipe Skiing: The sport of riding snow on a half-pipe, a U-shaped ramp. It became an Olympic event in 2014.

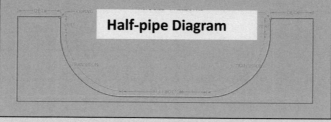

Half-pipe Diagram

Author: Dendowling

Mogul: A bump on a trail formed when skiers push the snow into mounds as they make turns.

Nordic Combined: A winter skiing event in which athletes compete in both cross-country skiing and ski jumping.

Slopestyle: A type of skiing (or snowboarding) in which athletes ski down a course that includes a variety of obstacles.

Snowboard

Big Air: A type of competition in which athletes perform tricks after launching off a jump built especially for the event.

Giant Slalom: A competition in which athletes navigate around series of poles spaced at a greater distance to each other than slalom.

Slalom: A competition in which athletes race by turning around gates in a set route.

ICE SPORTS

Curling

Curl: The curve the stone makes as it travels down the ice.

House (aka Rings): The circular scoring area.

Sheet: The playing area, which is 146 feet (44.5 meters) long.

Skip: The leader of a curling team.

Stone (aka Rock): The device – made out of granite and weighing 44 lb. (19.6 kg) – thrown by curlers during the game.

Ice Hockey

Goalie: Player who is responsible for guarding the goal against shots.

Hat Trick: Name used for the act of scoring three goals in one game.

Slap Shot: A shot in which a player swings aggressively through the puck, sending the shot at enormous speed toward the goal.

Figure Skating

Axel Jump: A jump in which the skater takes off facing forward, rotates 1.5 times in the air for a single Axel, 2.5 times for a double Axel, and 3.5 times for a triple Axel.

Salchow: A figure skating jump with a takeoff from the back inside edge of one skate followed by one or more turns in the air and landing on the back outside edge of the opposite skate.

Camel Spin: The skater spins on one leg with the free leg extended in the air, parallel to the ice.

Lutz: A jump in which the skater skates backwards in a big curve, then jumps and rotates in the air.

Quadruple Jump (aka Quad): A jump in which the skater completes four revolutions (or spins) in the air.

Speed Skating

Crossover: The step used by skaters in which they cross the outer foot over the inner to help maintain balance and speed in a curve.

Cross-Tracking: Term used when a skater crosses the path of another skater.

Sprint: A speed skating event of 500m or 1000m.

SLIDING SPORTS

Bobsled

Brakeman: The last person to enter the sled; responsible for pulling the brake to stop the sled at the end of the run.

Heat: A single run down a bobsled track.

Runners: The solid pieces of steel on which the sled rides.

Pilot: The driver of the sled; usually the first person to enter the sled.

Push Athlete: One of the two athletes in the middle of the sled in a four-man sled.

Luge

Block: The beginning of the start motion when the athlete rocks the sled forward.

Line: The fastest route down the track.

Luger: An athlete who competes in the sliding sport known as luge. The luger sleds face up and feet first.

Pod: The seat for the athlete.

Skeleton

Skeleton: A sliding sport in which an athletes rides a small sled down a frozen track while lying face down.

Toboggan: A term for the sled used in skeleton.

Medal Tracker
2018 Winter Olympics

SNOW SPORTS

ALPINE SKIING		Gold	Silver	Bronze	TOTAL
Downhill	Men				
Downhill	Women				
Super-G	Men				
Super-G	Women				
Giant Slalom	Men				
Giant Slalom	Women				
Slalom	Men				
Slalom	Women				
Alpine Combined	Men				
Alpine Combined	Women				
Team Event	Mixed				
TOTAL					

BIATHLON		Gold	Silver	Bronze	TOTAL
Sprint	Men				
Sprint	Women				
Pursuit	Men				
Pursuit	Women				
Individual	Men				
Individual	Women				
Mass Start	Men				
Mass Start	Women				
Relay	Men				
Relay	Women				
Mixed Relay	Mixed				
TOTAL					

SKI JUMPING		Gold	Silver	Bronze	TOTAL
Normal Hill	Men				
Normal Hill	Women				
Large Hill	Men				
Team	Men				
TOTAL					

CROSS-COUNTRY		Gold	Silver	Bronze	TOTAL
Individual	Men				
Individual	Women				
Skiathon	Men				
Skiathon	Women				
Sprint	Men				
Sprint	Women				
Team Sprint	Men				
Team Sprint	Women				
Mass Start	Men				
Mass Start	Women				
Relay	Men				
Relay	Women				
TOTAL					

FREESTYLE SKIING		Gold	Silver	Bronze	TOTAL
Moguls	Men				
Moguls	Women				
Aerials	Men				
Aerials	Women				
Ski Halfpipe	Men				
Ski Halfpipe	Women				
Ski Cross	Men				
Ski Cross	Women				
Ski Slopestyle	Men				
Ski Slopestyle	Women				
TOTAL					

SNOWBOARD		Gold	Silver	Bronze	TOTAL
Giant Slalom	Men				
Giant Slalom	Women				
Halfpipe	Men				
Halfpipe	Women				
Snowboard Cross	Men				
Snowboard Cross	Women				
Big Air	Men				
Big Air	Women				
Slopestyle	Men				
Slopestyle	Women				
TOTAL					

Medal Tracker, 2018 Winter Olympics

NORDIC COMBINED		Gold	Silver	Bronze	
Individual Normal	Men				
Individual Large	Men				
Team	Men				
TOTAL					

ICE SPORTS

CURLING		Gold	Silver	Bronze	TOTAL
Curling	Men				
Curling	Women				
Curling Mixed	Mixed				
TOTAL					

SPEED SKATING		Gold	Silver	Bronze	TOTAL
500 m	Men				
500 m	Women				
1000 m	Men				
10000 m	Women				
1500 m	Men				
1500 m	Women				
5000 m	Men				
3000 m	Women				
10000 m	Men				
5000 m	Women				
Mass Start	Men				
Mass Start	Women				
Team Pursuit	Men				
Team Pursuit	Women				
TOTAL					

Figure Skating		Gold	Silver	Bronze	TOTAL
Singles	Men				
Singles	Ladies				
Pair Skating	M & W				
Ice Dancing	M & W				
Team	M & W				
TOTAL					

ICE HOCKEY		Gold	Silver	Bronze	TOTAL
Tournament	Men				
Tournament	Women				
TOTAL					

SHORT TRACK		Gold	Silver	Bronze	TOTAL
Individual 500 m	Men				
Individual 500 m	Women				
Individual 1000 m	Men				
Individual 1000 m	Women				
Individual 1500 m	Men				
Individual 1500 m	Women				
Relay 5000 m	Men				
Relay 3000 m	Women				
TOTAL					

SLIDING SPORTS

BOBSLED		Gold	Silver	Bronze	TOTAL
4-man bobsled	Men				
2-man bobsled	Men				
Women's bobsled	Women				
TOTAL					

LUGE		Gold	Silver	Bronze	TOTAL
TOTAL	Men				
TOTAL	Women				
TOTAL	Doubles				
TOTAL	Team				
TOTAL					

SKELETON		Gold	Silver	Bronze	TOTAL
Skeleton	Men				
Skeleton	Women				
TOTAL					

Photo Credits and Source Notes

Photo Credits: Team USA Athletes

P. 17: Mikaela Shiffrin. U.S. Olympic Committee; P. 19: Susan Dunklee: U.S. Biathlon/Nordic Focus; P. 21: Jessie Diggins: U.S. Olympic Committee; P. 23: Gus Kenworthy: U.S. Olympic Committee; P. 25: Bryan Fletcher: U.S. Olympic Committee; P. 27: Sarah Hendrickson: U.S. Olympic Committee; P. 29: Jamie Anderson: U.S. Olympic Committee; P. 30: Alex Diebold: U.S. Olympic Committee; P. 33: John Shuster: USA Curling; P. 35: J.R. Celski: U.S. Speedskating; P. 37: Heather Bergsma: U.S. Speedskating; P. 39: Jocelyne Lamoureux-Davidson/Monique Lamoureux-Morando: U.S. Olympic Committee; P. 41: Nathan Chen: Hans Rosemond/U.S. Figure Skating; P. 42: Ashley Wagner: U.S. Olympic Committee; P. 45: Elana Meyer Taylor: Molly Choma; P. 47: Chris Mazdzer: USA Luge; P. 49: Katie Uhlaender: Molly Choma

Photo Credits: Miscellaneous

Page 8: Charles Jewtraw: Public Domain. **Page 13:** Olympic Cauldron, XXII Olympic Winter Games: www.kremlin.ru; Enriqueta Basilio: Public Domain; Yuna Kim: Public Domain. **Pages 16-48:** Pictograms of Olympic Sports: Public Domain. Author: Thadius856 (SVG conversion) and Parutakupiu (original image). **Page 16:** Alpine Skiing. Author: Jon Wick. **Page 18:** Biathlon. Jeremy Teela. U.S. Navy photo by Journalist lst Class Preston Keres. Public Domain. **Page 20:** Cross-country Skiing. Author: Bohringer Friedrich. **Page 22:** Freestyle Skiing. Author: 极博双板滑雪俱乐部 **Page 26:** Ski Jumping. Author: Taxiarchos228. Free Art License. **Page 28:** Snowboard: Author: Sōren. **Page 32:** Curling. 2006 Winter Olympic Games. Author: Bjarte Hetland. **Page 34:** Short Track. Author: Noelle Neu. **Page 36:** Speed Skating. Author: McSmit. **Page 43:** Bobsledders Vonetta Flower (left) and Jill Bakken (right): U.S. Navy photo by Journalist lst Class Preston Keres. Public Domain. **Page 44:** Bobsleigh. Public Domain. **Page 45:** Bobsleigh c. 1910: Author: Flyout (taken by ancestor of Flyout). **Page 46:** Luge. Author: Jon Wick. **Page 48:** Skeleton. Brady Canfield. Public Domain.

Source Notes

P. 17: Mikaela Shiffrin: "Being a great skier...." https://www.laureus.com/content/mikaela-shiffrin-interview; **P. 19: Susan Dunklee:** "The most important thing...." http://fasterskier.com/fsarticle/two-podium-newbies-dunklee-nove-mesto-top-three/. Retrieved 7/3/17; **P. 21: Jessie Diggins:** "It doesn't take a hero...." http://jessiediggins.com/the-last-3-races-in-europe/; **P. 23: Gus Kenworthy:** "When it snows...." http://guskenworthy.com/; **P. 25: Bryan Fletcher:** "As long as I have balance...." http://fasterskier.com/fsarticle/lillehammer-ostersund-west-notes-quotes/; **P. 27: Sarah Hendrickson**: "It is so easy...." http://go.teamusa.org/2sHpfNY; **P. 29: Jamie Anderson:** "I think with anything...." http://www.snowmagazine.com/features/1246-focus-on/interview-jamie-anderson; **P. 30: Alex Diebold:** "It's great to support...." https://www.usatoday.com/story/sports/olympics/sochi/2014/02/17/alex-deibold-wax-tech-snowboardcross/5554469/; **P. 33: John Shuster:** "My motivation really comes from...." http://www.startribune.com/olympic-curler-shuster-is-solid-as-a-rock-back-at-skip/241990751/; **P. 35: J.R. Celski:** "I thank God...." http://jrcelski.com/About; **P. 37: Heather Bergsma:** "I'm much more confident...." http://www.teamusa.org/News/2017/March/13/Meet-Speedskater-Heather-Bergsma-Who-Could-Win-More-Medals-Than-Any-Other-Athlete-In-2018; **P. 39: Monique Lamoureux-Morando: "If she's not...."** https://www.hockeywilderness.com/2014/1/24/5341562/team-usa-player-profiles-monique-and-jocelyne-lamoureux; **P. 41: Nathan Chen:** "There are a lot of cultural differences...." http://www.espn.com/olympics/figureskating/story/_/id/19017406/how-teen-figure-skater-nathan-chen-us-national-champion-spun-quad-jumps-gold; **P. 42: Ashley Wagner:** "My passion is what...." http://www.teamusa.org/News/2017/January/21/Karen-Chen-17-Overtakes-Several-Olympians-To-Win-First-US-Figure-Skating-Title; **P. 45: Elana Meyer Taylor**: "I love adventure...." http://www.11alive.com/news/local/downtown/olympian-elana-meyers-gives-gsu-commencement-speech/253128430; **P. 47: Chris Mazdzer:** "I've failed a lot...." http://newsroom.devry.edu/in-the-news/devry-university-student-athlete-chris-mazdzer-featured-in-waxahachie-newspapers.htm; **P. 48: Katie Uhlaender:** "Being an Olympian is a huge...." http://www.beliefnet.com/entertainment/olympic-games/katie-uhlaender-interview.aspx#HD9Z5Syz5DS3BkpC.99

A Kid's Guide to
The 2018 Winter Games
For Parents and Teachers

About This Book

A Kid's Guide to the 2018 Winter Games is part of a series of engaging, easy-to-read nonfiction books for young readers. The series focuses primarily on countries and culture around the world but also includes special editions on current and timely topics, such as the 2018 Winter Games. Each book in the series features captivating full-color photographs, informational charts and graphs, and quirky and bizarre "Did You Know" facts, all designed to bring the topic to life. Designed primarily for recreational, high-interest reading, the informational text series is also a great resource for students to use to research geography topics or writing assignments.

About the Reading Level

A Kid's Guide to . . . is an informational text series designed for kids in grades 4 to 6, ages 9 to 12. For some young readers, the series will provide new reading challenges based on the vocabulary and sentence structure. For other readers, the series will reinforce reading skills already mastered. While for still other readers, the series text will match their current skill level, regardless of age or grade level.

About the Author

Jack L. Roberts is the co-founder and publisher of Curious Kids Press, an educational book publishing company focusing on nonfiction titles for young readers. Roberts began his career in educational publishing at Children's Television Workshop (now Sesame Workshop), where he was Senior Editor of The Sesame Street/Electric Company Reading Kits. Later, at Scholastic Inc., he was the founding editor of a high-interest/low-reading level magazine for middle school students. He is also the author of more than a dozen biographies and other non-fiction titles for young readers, published by Scholastic Inc., the Lerner Publishing Group, Teacher Created Materials, and Benchmark Education. More recently, he was the co-founder of WordTeasers, an educational series of card decks designed to help kids of all ages improve their vocabulary through "conversation, not memorization."

Other Books from Curious Kids Press

www.curiouskidspress.com

For Beginning Readers

Available as E-book or Print Edition!

Curious Kids Press

The Elephant Picture Book

With original photography of the elephants at Boon Lott's Elephant Sanctuary in Thailand.

Ages 4-7

By Jack L. Roberts
With Photography
by Michael Owens